Marilyn

A LIFE IN PICTURES

Marilyn
A LIFE IN PICTURES

Diana Karanikas Harvey

MetroBooks

MetroBooks

An Imprint of Friedman/Fairfax Publishers

Library of Congress Cataloging-in-Publication Data

Harvey, Diana Karanikas.
       Marilyn: a life in pictures / Diana Karanikas Harvey.
             p. cm.
       Filmography: p.
       Includes bibliographical references and index.
       ISBN 1-56799-774-0
       1. Monroe, Marilyn, 1926–1962—Portraits. I. Title.
PN2287.M69H34   1999
791.43'028'092—dc21   98-47387

ISBN 1-56799-774-0

Editor: Steven Pettingill
Art Director: Jeff Batzli
Designer: Meredith Miller
Photography Editor: Amy Talluto

Color separations by Ocean Graphic International Company Ltd.
Printed in China by Leefung-Asco Printers Ltd.

3 5 7 9 10 8 6 4

For bulk purchases and special sales, please contact:
Friedman/Fairfax Publishers
Attention: Sales Department
15 West 26th Street
New York, NY 10010
212/685-6610   FAX 212/685-1307

Visit our website:
http://www.metrobooks.com

Acknowledgments

Very special thanks to Jackson Harvey, Matt Leipzig, Francine Hornberger,
Steven Pettingill, and to George Leis, without whom I'd still be using DOS.

Dedication

This book is dedicated with love to my parents, Alexander and Helen
Karanikas, who taught me how to write.

CONTENTS

Introduction

Above: "When you think of the American Way of Life, everyone thinks of chewing gum, Coca-Cola and Marilyn Monroe."
—from the Russian magazine *Nedyela*

Opposite: Marilyn's unique combination of sensuality and vulnerability has captivated the imaginations of countless fans for half a century.

Right: Marilyn Monroe epitomizes the glamour and allure of Hollywood.

Opposite: "I used to think as I looked out on the Hollywood night, 'There must be thousands of girls sitting alone like me, dreaming of becoming a movie star. But I'm not going to worry about them. I'm dreaming the hardest.'"
—Marilyn Monroe

Marilyn Monroe is a Hollywood icon. Her image is plastered throughout every souvenir shop on Hollywood Boulevard. Tourists from around the world snatch up her memorabilia, and have their photos taken while standing next to a life-size cardboard image of her. She is more recognized and well-loved than a great deal of today's movie stars. All this, for an actress who died more than thirty-five years ago. What is it about Marilyn Monroe that still captures the imaginations of so many people?

Norma Jean Baker, A.K.A. Marilyn Monroe, came from humble beginnings. She bounced between orphanages and foster homes, and was left with an overwhelming desire to be wanted and loved. She rose to stardom as a sex symbol in the 1950s, and in a time characterized by "Ozzie and Harriet" conservative social mores, Marilyn wore plunging necklines and posed nude for the camera. She was married three times, divorced three times, and cavorted with some of the most famous and influential men of the century—married or not. But she was never shunned by the press

or the public. In fact, every scandal she was involved in only served to make her more popular. Her life had the makings of a soap opera Cinderella story, except the ending—when she died tragically, at age thirty-six, of an overdose of sleeping pills. And though some have theorized otherwise, the heroine of this story was most likely the victim of her unhappiness, brought on by her fractured identity. In any case, with her death, a legend was born—the legend that is now and forever Marilyn Monroe.

Now she stands, a symbol—the reigning goddess in a mythical city—not so much of what Hollywood actually was, but of our perception of how it must have been. Perhaps she is still so popular because this illusion is so important to us. Her story is meaningful to us, perhaps now more than ever, because, among the tawdry storefronts and the cynical malcontents who now have the run of the once-glorious boulevard, she remains unchanged—forever glamorous, forever beautiful, forever young.

Chapter One

A Starlet Is Born

Above: Norma Jean Baker was born on June 1, 1926. Her mother, Gladys Baker Mortensen, unable to care for the child she had had out of wedlock, boarded Norma Jean with a neighboring family—the strict and religious Ida and Wayne Bolender. Norma Jean never knew her father, believed to be C. Stanley Gifford, a salesman at the same Hollywood film lab where Gladys was employed. As an adult, Norma Jean tried to contact Gifford, but he refused to speak with her, even when she called as Marilyn Monroe.

Opposite: "Don't worry, Norma Jean. You're going to be a beautiful girl when you grow up. I can feel it in my bones." —Grace McKee Goddard, Norma Jean's legal guardian

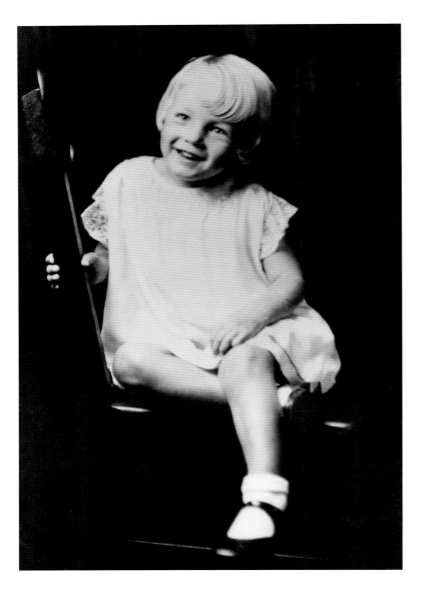

Left: When she was six, Norma Jean moved in with her mother, Gladys, who worked double shifts to afford a small bungalow that she decorated in white and outfitted with a piano for her daughter to play. This time period was one of the few pleasant memories of Norma Jean's childhood. White would forever be her favorite color. Her happiness, however, was short-lived. Only three months after Norma Jean moved in, Gladys suffered a nervous breakdown and was institutionalized. Norma Jean was taken in by Grace McKee (later Goddard), her mother's best friend. But when Grace married, the young Norma Jean was dragged, literally, to an orphanage. She spent several years bouncing between foster homes and the orphanage until the age of eleven, when Goddard moved Norma Jean into the home of Ana Lower, Goddard's aunt. Marilyn later said, "There's only one person in the world I ever loved. That was Aunt Ana."

Below: On June 19, 1942, at the age of sixteen, Norma Jean was married to Jim Dougherty (here pictured), a twenty-one-year-old employed by Lockhead Aviation. The courtship had been plotted by Norma Jean's legal guardian, Grace Goddard, who was leaving Los Angeles and felt marriage would be the best means of providing a secure situation for the teenage Norma Jean. Marilyn remembered her arranged marriage differently: "Again, it was the case of not being wanted."

ight: Norma Jean and first
husband Jim Dougherty. In
1944, despite Norma Jean's
pleading, Dougherty enlisted in
the Merchant Marine and was
soon after sent to Shanghai.
While he was overseas, Norma
Jean began modeling, and
her dream of being an actress
was born. Her burgeoning success as a model, Jim's dis-
approval of her new career
aspirations, and his extended
absence led Norma Jean to file
for divorce. On September 13,
1946, their marriage was dis-
solved. Dougherty said in 1976,
"If I hadn't gone into the
Merchant Marine during World
War Two, she would still be
Mrs. Dougherty today."

Right: Norma Jean was working at the Radio Plane Company in Burbank when she was "discovered" by David Conover, a photographer who was visiting the plant to take "morale-booster" photos for World War II soldiers. When he passed by Norma Jean, he said, "You're a real morale booster." The photos he took appeared in hundreds of U.S. Army camp publications and were the first ever images of Norma Jean/Marilyn to appear in print. Conover introduced his find to Emmeline Snively, head of the Blue Book Talent Agency (at the time the largest modeling agency in Los Angeles), and in the summer of 1945, Norma Jean signed her first agency contract.

Opposite: It was Norma Jean's first agent, Emmeline Snively, who convinced the young model to bleach her hair. Marilyn recalled Snively's words, "If you ever want to go places, you've got to be a blonde."

Above: Once she started modeling bathing suits, Norma Jean's career took off. She appeared in (and on the cover of) numerous magazines, including *Laff*, *Peak*, and *See*. Howard Hughes, then owner of RKO Studios, saw Norma Jean's image, and demanded that his studio give the cover girl a screen test. Emmeline Snively used Hughes' interest to nab her client a meeting with Ben Lyon, a talent scout with a rival studio, Twentieth Century Fox. Lyon arranged a silent, color screen test for Norma Jean. On August 16, 1946, the twenty-year-old signed a standard player contract with Twentieth Century Fox.

Below: In this cheesecake shot, Marilyn prepares to "go skating." Another of Marilyn's early duties as a Fox starlet, in addition to posing for these photos, was riding on a float in a parade. She had just changed her name from Norma Jean Dougherty, and when someone watching the parade wanted her autograph, she had to ask, "How do you spell Marilyn Monroe?"

Above: As Fox's new starlet, Marilyn's first assignments for the movie studio were not films, but so-called "cheesecake shots," titillating still photos of the actress, usually involved in some activity and always scantily clad. In this cheesecake shot, Marilyn "plays ball."

Above: During her year with Fox, Marilyn appeared only as a bit player in two films, *Scudda-Hoo! Scudda-Hay!* and *Dangerous Years*. Here, she is pictured in *Dangerous Years* as Eve, a waitress in a teen jukebox parlor. Her contract option at Fox was dropped several weeks after the filming of *Dangerous Years*, on August 25, 1947, and Marilyn suddenly found herself unemployed.

Opposite: In March 1948, Marilyn signed a contract with Columbia Pictures. The studio gave her her first co-starring role, in a low-budget musical entitled *Ladies of the Chorus*.

Below: Here, Marilyn performs a scene with Adele Jergens in the 1949 Columbia Pictures film *Ladies of the Chorus*. As preparation for the musical, Marilyn took acting lessons from Natasha Lytess and voice lessons from Fred Karger. Lytess became Marilyn's personal drama coach, omnipresent on the actress' movie sets. Karger became romantically involved with the starlet, but saw her as neither wife nor mother material and balked when she suggested marriage. She later referred to him on several occasions as her first love.

Above: Marilyn Monroe as one of the "ladies of the chorus." This was the only movie in which she actually acted while with Columbia Studios. Her only other appearance in a Columbia film was in a western—Gene Autry serenaded her photograph. Her contract option was dropped after a mere six months and in September 1948, Marilyn was, once again, out of work.

Right: Marilyn had been out of work for six months in 1949 when her agent, Harry Lipton, set up an audition for Groucho Marx, who was casting for a bit part in his upcoming film, *Love Happy*. Marx was looking for a starlet who could "walk by me in such a manner as to arouse my elderly libido and cause smoke to issue from my ears." He found his girl in Marilyn Monroe. Said Marilyn of *Love Happy*, "No acting, just sex again. I had to wiggle across a room. I practiced jiggling my backside for a week. Groucho loved it."

Above: Marilyn, pictured in 1949, as a chorus girl in *A Ticket to Tomahawk*, another bit part in a mediocre film.

Opposite: William Morris super-agent Johnny Hyde saw an advance screening of *Love Happy*, and was taken with the twenty-two-year-old Monroe. After meeting with her at the Palm Springs Racquet Club, Hyde became Marilyn's new agent. The two became lovers, and the ailing fifty-three-year-old Hyde desperately wanted to marry Marilyn. But even after Hyde's wife divorced him because of the all-too-public affair, Marilyn continued to reject his repeated offers of marriage. Her rejection did nothing to wane the fervor with which he promoted her career, and Johnny Hyde is ultimately the figure most credited with having made Marilyn Monroe a star.

Below: Johnny Hyde, Marilyn's agent/lover, was intent upon making Marilyn a star. Through his relentless promotion, Marilyn finally landed an acting role in a quality film, *The Asphalt Jungle*. Marilyn played Angela Finlay, the mistress of influential lawyer Alonzo D. Emmerich (Louis Calhern). Here she is pictured with Calhern.

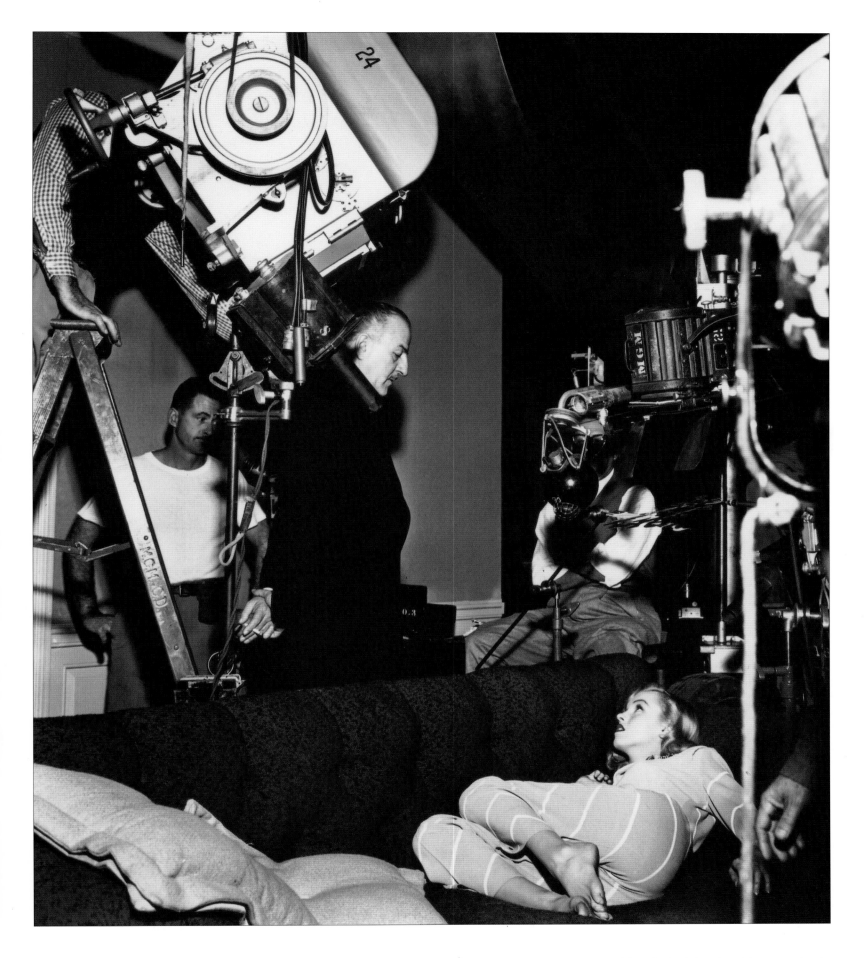

Above: Marilyn on the set of *The Asphalt Jungle*, with costar Louis Calhern, who had already won two Academy Awards at the time. Said Huston, "I was far more taken with her in the flesh than on the screen when we first worked together. I had no idea she'd go so far so fast."

Left: A poster for the 1950 MGM release *The Asphalt Jungle*. The classic noir film about a jewelry heist and the corruption of those involved—both the cops and the crooks—was Marilyn's first important film role.

Below: "There's a beautiful blonde, too, name of Marilyn Monroe, who plays Calhern's girlfriend, and makes the most of her footage."
—*Photoplay* review of *The Asphalt Jungle*.

bove: Marilyn in a scene from *The Asphalt Jungle*. When the superb movie was released in 1950, the public began to take notice of Marilyn Monroe and so did Hollywood. For the first time in her career, producers actually began to offer her roles without an audition.

Opposite: The culmination of her first five years in show business: Marilyn Monroe was voted "Miss Cheesecake" of 1951.

Above: Marilyn with (from left) Anne Baxter, Bette Davis, and George Sanders in the 1950 Twentieth Century Fox classic, *All About Eve*. The film went on to win several Academy Awards, including Best Picture. Marilyn's work in the film earned her a new contract with Fox, at $750 per week. Johnny Hyde negotiated the terms of the agreement, and it would be the last deal he ever made for the starlet. Marilyn's agent/lover/mentor died of heart disease on December 18, 1950. At Hyde's funeral, Marilyn threw herself upon his coffin and screamed, "Wake up, please wake up, oh my God, Johnny, Johnny."

Right: In 1951, Marilyn was once again under contract with Twentieth Century Fox. Only this time, the studio launched a massive publicity campaign to promote her, and Marilyn would soon go from starlet to star. Initially, however, it took Fox months to find a suitable part for her, opting, as they had under her previous contract, for rounds of cheesecake still photos and personal appearances. The byline for this photo reads, "Not a shadow of a chance for any waistline bulging to set in here. Marilyn keeps trim, healthy, and curvaceous just by romping like a schoolgirl over the green grass in bare feet."

Chapter Two

The Monroe Doctrine

Opposite: Fox took several months to find an appropriate film vehicle for Marilyn. In the meantime, she was loaned out to MGM, for a role in *Hometown Story*. She played Miss Martin, a secretary in a newspaper office.

Above: "She comes out of the dressing room Norma Jean. When she stepped in front of the camera, she was Marilyn."
—Lawrence Schiller

Left: In 1950, Marilyn appeared in the MGM flop *Right Cross*, in a bit part as the girlfriend of Dick Powell (pictured here). Marilyn's name is not even mentioned in the film's credits.

Right: In 1951, Twentieth Century Fox began a massive promotional campaign to launch their new starlet, Marilyn Monroe, or, as they dubbed her, "The Cinderella of Hollywood."

Left: Marilyn in *Hometown Story*, with Jeffrey Lynn. The *Variety* review claimed Marilyn was "up to script demands."

Right: Fox began a rapid-fire succession of films as vehicles for Marilyn in late 1951. Here, she is pictured in the first, *As Young As You Feel*, with Albert Dekker. This film marked the first time Marilyn's name was placed on theater marquees.

Opposite: Marilyn and Jack Paar in a publicity photo for the 1951 film *Love Nest*. In the movie she plays an ex-WAC whose presence causes trouble for a married couple (played by Willliam Lundigan and June Haver). Paar plays a lecherous attorney.

Right: On the set during the filming of *Love Nest*, Marilyn takes the bobby pins out of her hair.

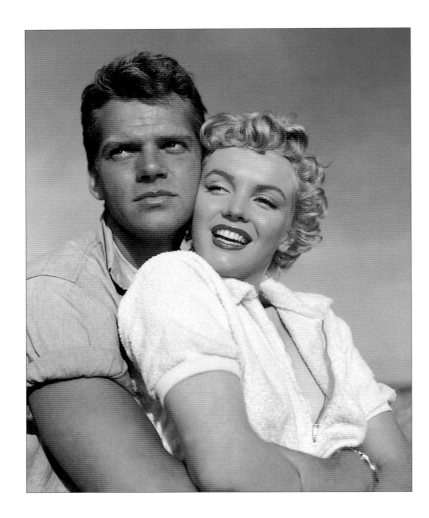

Above: Marilyn with Keith Andes in the 1952 RKO film *Clash by Night*. Her most important role to date garnered her co-star billing and the best reviews she had yet received. A series of nude calendar photos she had done several years earlier became public prior to the release of *Clash by Night*, and Marilyn was more popular than ever. The film was a box office smash.

Right: Marilyn in *Let's Make It Legal* (1951), with (from left) MacDonald Carey, Zachary Scott, and Claudette Colbert. Monroe plays a gold digger seeking a rich husband at a posh hotel. During filming, she was harshly chastised by director Richard Sale when she showed up forty-five minutes late, keeping Claudette Colbert waiting. Her tardiness would become a recurrent problem throughout her career.

Left: In *We're Not Married* (1952), Marilyn and David Wayne (pictured here) play one of five couples who discover they were never legally married—the Justice of the Peace who performed their ceremony hadn't yet received his license. Other members of the stellar cast in this episodic film include Ginger Rogers, Fred Allen, Eve Arden, Paul Douglas, Mitzi Gaynor, Eddie Bracken, Louis Calhern, and Zsa Zsa Gabor.

Opposite: Marilyn receives the title of Mrs. Mississippi in *We're Not Married*. When she discovers her marriage to her husband Jeff (David Wayne) was never legal, she goes on to compete for and win the title of *Miss* Mississippi while he stays home and takes care of their baby. Said the New York *Herald Tribune* of the movie, "With David Wayne and Marilyn Monroe (who looks as though she had been carved out of cake by Michelangelo), it becomes a reason for a kitchen-bound husband to demand that his wife drop her busy activities as a beauty contest winner and return to the home."

Opposite: The 1952 melodrama *Don't Bother to Knock* marked Marilyn's first starring role for Fox, as a psychotic baby-sitter. The reviews were, at best, mixed. Said the New York *Post*, "In *Don't Bother to Knock*, at the Globe, they've thrown Marilyn Monroe into the deep dramatic waters, sink or swim, and while she doesn't really do either, you might say that she floats. With that figure what else can she do, and what would be better?"

Above: Marilyn as the psychotic Nell in *Don't Bother to Knock*. While the film garnered poor reviews, Marilyn herself felt she had done some of her finest work and, reportedly, did not require a single retake during filming.

Left: Marilyn returned to comedy with the madcap film *Monkey Business* (1952). Monroe plays a secretary who can't type. Here she is pictured with co-star Cary Grant.

Right: With Cary Grant in *Monkey Business*. The New York *Daily News* complimented Marilyn's performance by claiming she could "look and act dumber than any of the screen's current blondes."

Above: Cary Grant, Ginger Rogers, and Marilyn Monroe in Howard Hawks' *Monkey Business*. Despite all the talent involved, the film was best described by the New York *Daily News* as "amusing nonsense." Even with the lukewarm reviews, it still performed fairly well at the box office.

Left: Marilyn manhandles Cary Grant in *Monkey Business*. *Photoplay* wrote, "Marilyn Monroe garners laughs and whistles, bouncing in and out as a secretary who can't type. Typing skill, however, is the only attribute which the lady appears to be lacking in."

Left: In November 1952, Marilyn was a guest on the Edgar Bergen/ Charlie McCarthy radio show, one of the most popular variety programs of the time.

Below: Marilyn plays the sexy/adulterous/murderous wife of Joseph Cotten (here pictured) in the 1953 film *Niagara*. While reviews were mixed, the film was a huge box office success. Marilyn's performance in the role of Rose Loomis in the Hitchock-style thriller launched her to stardom.

Opposite: Marilyn as Rose Loomis in *Niagara*. In the script, she is described as the kind of wife whose dress is "cut so low you can see her knees." Perhaps the most provocative shot in the film is that of Marilyn walking away from the camera, in a tight skirt, with a seductive gait, while the camera remains focused on her behind. At the time, it was the longest screen walk ever—a daring shot for 1953 and a classic Marilyn Monroe moment.

Marilyn MONROE Joseph COTTEN Jean PETERS

niagara

TECHNICOLOR

CON CASEY ADAMS · DENIS O'DEA · RICHARD ALLAN
DON WILSON · LURENE TUTTLE · RUSSELL COLLINS
WILL WRIGHT

UNA PRODUZIONE DI **CHARLES BRACKETT**
REGIA DI **HENRY HATHAWAY**
SCENEGGIATURA DI Charles BRACKETT · Walter REISCH · Richard BREEN

20th CENTURY FOX

G. SCARPATI S.p.A. · Napoli 1960 N. 3631

Left: The poster for the film *Niagara*. Marilyn enchanted viewers with her singing of "Kiss."

Opposite: From *Niagara*, a passionate screen embrace with Ted Patrick (played by Richard Allan), Rose's partner in love and murder.

Above: With director Henry Hathaway on the set of *Niagara*. Hathaway's direction coupled with Joe MacDonald's cinematography showcased Marilyn's sultry presence. *The New York Times* review read, "Perhaps Miss Monroe is not the perfect actress at this point. But neither the director nor the gentlemen who handled the cameras appeared to be concerned with this. They have caught every possible curve both in the intimacy of the boudoir and in equally revealing tight dresses. And they have illustrated pretty concretely that she can be seductive—even when she walks."

Opposite: In *Niagara*, Marilyn proved her overwhelming on-screen and box-office appeal.

ight: Marilyn Monroe and Jane Russell in *Gentlemen Prefer Blondes*. Among the memorable musical numbers were "Two Little Girls from Little Rock" (Jule Styne and Leo Robin), "When Love Goes Wrong" (Hoagy Carmichael and Harold Adamson), "Bye Bye Baby" (Jule Styne and Leo Robin), and Marilyn's show-stopping solo number, "Diamonds Are a Girl's Best Friend" (Jule Styne and Leo Robin).

elow: Marilyn Monroe with Jane Russell and Elliot Reed in *Gentlemen Prefer Blondes*. Darryl Zanuck, the head of Twentieth Century Fox, saw a preview of the film and released the following statement to the press: "If anyone has any doubts as to the future of Marilyn Monroe, *Gentlemen Prefer Blondes* is the answer."

Below: Marilyn, with George Winslow, in a scene from *Gentlemen Prefer Blondes*. The New York *Herald Tribune* review proclaimed, "As usual, Miss Monroe looks as though she would glow in the dark, and her version of the baby-faced blonde whose eyes open for diamonds and close for kisses is always amusing as well as alluring."

Left: Diamonds are a girl's best friend—Marilyn displays the goods in *Gentlemen Prefer Blondes*.

Right: Marilyn, Charles Coburn, and Jane Russell celebrate resounding success at a party for the premiere of *Gentlemen Prefer Blondes*.

Right: The 1953 musical *Gentlemen Prefer Blondes*, directed by Howard Hawks, was Marilyn's ticket to superstardom. As Lorelei Lee, a nightclub singer and dancer, Monroe lit up the screen, and created her most enduring on-screen persona.

Below: Marilyn on the set of *Gentlemen Prefer Blondes*, with her acting coach, Natasha Lytess.

Right: On June 28, 1953, Marilyn and Jane Russell stamped their handprints into immortality in front of Grauman's Chinese Theatre. Extra police were needed to control the traffic amid the hordes of newspeople and wolf-whistling fans.

Above: Marilyn, Lauren Bacall, and Betty Grable sitting pretty in the 1953 Twentieth Century Fox film *How to Marry a Millionaire*. The movie was the second ever to be shot in CinemaScope (*The Robe* was the first). The plot revolves around the adventures of three women who rent an expensive Manhattan apartment and scheme to marry themselves to millionaires.

Opposite: Marilyn with Betty Grable in *How to Marry a Millionaire*. The two most famous Fox blondes were paired up for the comedy and, while industry insiders predicted fireworks, the actresses worked together with no evident friction on- or off-screen.

Above: Rory Calhoun, Lauren Bacall, Cameron Mitchell and Marilyn in *How to Marry a Millionaire*. Prior to filming, Marilyn objected to playing the part of Pola because she didn't want to wear glasses. However, director Jean Negulesco convinced her it was the best role and she acquiesced.

Right: The poster for *How to Marry a Millionaire*. Said the New York *Herald Tribune* upon seeing Marilyn in CinemaScope, "The big question, 'How does Marilyn Monroe looked stretched across a broad screen?' is easily answered. If you insisted on sitting in the front row, you would probably feel as though you were being smothered in baked Alaska."

Above: Lauren Bacall, Humphrey Bogart, and Marilyn in 1953, at the premiere of *How to Marry a Millionaire*.

Above: "It's like a good double play combination. It's just a matter of two people meeting and something clicks."
—Joe DiMaggio on meeting Marilyn

When Marilyn met Joe DiMaggio in 1952, he was retired from baseball, but he had made his mark as one of the greatest ever to play the game. Joltin' Joe led the New York Yankees to ten World Series championships, made the record books by hitting in fifty-six consecutive games in 1941, and was the first player in history to make $100,000 per year. After their initial date, Marilyn is claimed to have said about Joe, "He struck out." However, DiMaggio was persistent, phoning Marilyn every day for more than two weeks until he finally won her over. Marilyn and Joe became a couple, and a more popular union—in the eyes of the press and the public—could hardly be imagined. They were the hottest celebrity couple of their time.

Opposite: On January 14, 1954, Marilyn and Joe DiMaggio were married in the office of Municipal Judge Charles Peery in San Francisco. Newsmen were excluded from the simple ceremony, but the couple were besieged by throngs of reporters as they left the courthouse.

Above: Marilyn, recently married to Joe DiMaggio, interrupted her honeymoon in February 1954 to entertain American troops in Korea. She flew into Seoul via helicopter and was met by thousands of cheering soldiers.

Right: Servicemen traveled from all points of the Korean peninsula to see Marilyn perform in Seoul. She sang several numbers, including "Diamonds Are a Girl's Best Friend," and "Somebody Love Me." In four days, she performed ten shows for more than 100,000 frenzied troops. The soldiers of the Forty-fifth Infantry Division became so riled up that a rock-throwing riot ensued. Marilyn appreciated the adulation: "I never felt like a star before in my heart."

Above: Marilyn, visiting American troops in Korea, says good-bye to Donald Wakehouse, the last repatriate from "Operation Big Switch," after signing his hipcast: "Love and kisses, Marilyn Monroe."

Left: With Robert Mitchum in *River of No Return* (1954). The movie, directed by Otto Preminger, was Marilyn's first western.

Below: Marilyn rests on the set of *River of No Return*. *The New York Times* review stated, "The mountainous scenery is spectacular, but so, in her own way, is Miss Monroe."

*R*ight: *There's No Business Like Show Business* (1954) was a film tribute to composer Irving Berlin. While Marilyn sizzled on screen in numbers like "Heat Wave," her marriage to Joe DiMaggio began to deteriorate during the shoot (Marilyn made the film against DiMaggio's wishes). Marilyn reportedly collapsed on the set three times.

*B*elow: Tommy Rettig and Marilyn in *River of No Return*. Marilyn wasn't pleased with the film: "Knowing what I know now, I wouldn't accept *River of No Return*. I think I deserve a better deal than a 'Z' cowboy movie, in which the acting finishes third to the scenery and CinemaScope."

Opposite: *The Seven Year Itch*, with its explicitly sexual scenes (for 1955), became the last film Marilyn would do as Mrs. DiMaggio. Along with about 4,000 gawking New Yorkers, Joe watched the filming of the most famous scene, where Marilyn stands over a subway grating, obviously enjoying the breeze that blows up her white diaphanous dress. The day after the scene was shot, DiMaggio returned to California alone. The two were divorced soon after.

ight: Marilyn as The Girl in *The Seven Year Itch*. She is the neighbor and fantasy object of Richard Sherman (Tom Ewell, pictured), a man whose wife (of seven years) and son are away on summer vacation.

Above: On October 27, 1954, Marilyn and Joe DiMaggio, once the most celebrated couple in Hollywood, agreed to a divorce. In the months after the split, DiMaggio tried to reconcile, and even hired a private detective to follow his ex-wife, which ultimately resulted in the infamous "Wrong Door Raid." On November 5, 1954, convinced by private eye Barney Ruditsky that his ex-wife was committing some illicit act in one of the Waring Apartments, DiMaggio (accompanied by his friend Frank Sinatra) decided to "raid" the suite Marilyn was supposedly in. It was the wrong apartment. The tenant later sued the two stars for $200,000, though the lawsuit was settled for $7,500. After the incident, the couple still tried to reconcile and, on June 1, 1955, DiMaggio accompanied Marilyn to the premiere of *The Seven Year Itch* (pictured here). After the screening, DiMaggio threw a birthday party for Marilyn, but the couple reportedly fought later in the evening and failed to reunite. While they never re-married, they also never fully left each other; Marilyn and Joe remained friends and on-and-off partners for the rest of her life.

Above: After the huge success of *The Seven Year Itch* (it grossed $8 million at the box office), Marilyn was awarded a new contract with Twentieth Century Fox. She was allowed director and cinematographer approval, a personal maid, and was to be paid no less than $100,000 a picture with an additional $500 per week for incidental expenses. Her deal also stipulated that she would only be given class "A" movies. The terms of her fourth contract with Fox, which she signed on December 31, 1955, were unprecedented at the time and presumed Marilyn to be the top movie idol in Hollywood.

Chapter Three

Twilight of the Goddess

A bove: *Some Like It Hot* (1959) was Marilyn's most financially successful film and arguably the most popular motion picture comedy ever. The movie was number one at the box office for three months, received rave reviews, and won Marilyn a Golden Globe Award for Best Actress. Behind the scenes, however, Marilyn was not just difficult, she was impossible, and her antics created rifts among the cast and crew.

O pposite: "When I saw her up there, it was nearly incredible. The legend, which I thought was a kind of joke in questionable taste, suddenly made sense. I could understand why all the fuss had been made, why the crowds went out of their minds whenever they caught a glimpse of her. It's a kind of magic."

—Angela Allen, director John Huston's longtime script supervisor

Above: Marilyn in 1955 with friends (from left to right), Jacques Cernas, Sammy Davis, Jr., Milton Greene, and Mel Torme.

Left: Marilyn and Marlon Brando, in New York attending a benefit dinner for the Actors Studio, 1955. Marilyn took time off from Hollywood to study "The Method" style of acting at the acclaimed Actors Studio. Lee Strasberg, head of the studio, became Marilyn's friend and mentor; his wife Paula became her private coach; and Brando, another student at the time, was rumored to be her lover.

Left: Following her studies at the Actors Studio in New York, Marilyn returned to Hollywood a "more serious actress." Known for her plunging necklines, she set the fashion world agog with her conservative, almost mannish suit, which she wore with a black shirt and tie. Monroe declared she was just the same old Marilyn, in a new suit.

ight: On the bus in the 1956 film adaptation of the William Inge play *Bus Stop*. Arguably Marilyn's best performance, the film validated her lucrative new Fox contract, her studies of "The Method" style of acting in New York, and her work with her new on-set drama coach, Paula Strasberg.

pposite: Marilyn began dating the brilliant playwright Arthur Miller in 1955 when she was in New York. Miller, along with Tennessee Williams, shared the position of most influential playwright of his time—he won the New York Drama Critics Circle Award for *All My Sons*, and the Pulitzer Prize for *Death of a Salesman*. His liaison with Marilyn was, at first, secret because Miller was married. But in 1956, he divorced his wife, left his children, and joined Monroe in Los Angeles. The press was astonished by the seemingly odd couple, and dubbed Miller and Marilyn "The Egghead and the Hourglass."

elow: With Don Murray in Joshua Logan's movie, *Bus Stop*. The *New York Times* review proclaimed, "Hold on to your chairs, everybody, and get set for a rattling surprise. Marilyn Monroe has finally proved herself an actress in *Bus Stop*."

Left: Marilyn and Arthur Miller in front of his summer home in Roxbury, Connecticut, 1956. Said Marilyn at the time, "We're so congenial. This is the first time I've been really in love. Arthur is a serious man, but he has a wonderful sense of humor. We laugh and joke a lot. I'm mad about him." Marilyn and Miller were married in two ceremonies—a civic ceremony on June 29, 1956, and a Jewish wedding on July 1, 1956.

Left: "I've promised myself never to let Marilyn Monroe get in the way of Mr. and Mrs. Miller." Marilyn signs an autograph for a fan as husband Arthur Miller looks on.

Right: In the 1957 film *The Prince and the Showgirl*, Marilyn starred with and was directed by Laurence Olivier. In the film, Marilyn plays an American chorus girl attempting to melt the heart of a stuffy Prince Regent (Olivier). The film received mixed reviews and average box office attendance at the time, but is now considered one of Marilyn's best efforts.

Above: Marilyn and Laurence Olivier quickly grew to resent each other during the shoot of *The Prince and The Showgirl*. Olivier disapproved of Marilyn's customary lateness and her dependence on acting coach Paula Strasberg—who was eventually banished from the set altogether. By the end of the shoot, the two stars were barely speaking.

Marilyn Monroe · Laurence Olivier
The Prince and the Showgirl

TECHNICOLOR® A FILM BY MARILYN MONROE PRODUCTIONS, INC. AND L.O.P. LTD. PRESENTED BY WARNER BROS.

eft: Tony Curtis and Marilyn in *Some Like It Hot*. The two stars did not like each other and feuded on the set. In public, Curtis denounced Marilyn's unprofessional behavior, proclaimed he would never work with her again, and lambasted her with comments like, "Kissing her is like kissing Hitler," and "I think Marilyn is as mad as a hatter." For her part, Marilyn kept her dislike of Curtis a private matter.

elow: With Jack Lemmon in *Some Like It Hot*. At first, Marilyn was angry that Jack won the role over her friend Frank Sinatra, but eventually, she grew to like Lemmon. Her behavior on the set was hardly likable—she was late or she didn't show up at all, and her growing dependence on sleeping pills was causing her to forget her lines. To the exasperation of director Billy Wilder, it took her forty-seven takes to knock on a door and deliver the line, "It's me, sugar."

pposite, bottom: The poster for *The Prince and the Showgirl*. As producer, Marilyn gave herself top billing over Laurence Olivier, by far the more accomplished actor. The fact that Olivier directed the movie isn't even mentioned on the poster, possibly because of the disrespect the British actor showed for Marilyn during the shoot (for instance, he once referred to her as "a professional amateur").

Below: Marilyn, Jack Lemmon, and Tony Curtis discuss a shot during the filming of *Some Like It Hot*. The timing of every scene in this movie is so perfect it's difficult to believe that Marilyn was so haywire off-screen; much of the credit for the film's excellence is due to master director Billy Wilder.

Left: With Yves Montand in *Let's Make Love* (1960). Even though both stars were married at the time, she to Miller and he to Simone Signoret, Montand and Marilyn became lovers. *Let's Make Love* was Marilyn's twenty-seventh film and one of her least successful ventures, despite the uncredited script rewrite by her Pulitzer Prize-winning husband Arthur Miller and the presence of brilliant comedy director George Cukor. Her use of sleeping pills had become so prolific that her eyes appear bloodshot throughout the film.

Below: Marilyn and Yves Montand at a cocktail party in January 1960. Their affair was highly publicized, as was Marilyn's announcement that she was divorcing Arthur Miller. While her divorce would go through, Montand would never leave his wife, Simone Signoret. When the affair was over, the French star called Marilyn unsophisticated, a "simple girl," and stated, "Perhaps she had a schoolgirl crush. If she did, I'm sorry. But, nothing will break up my marriage."

Left: Marilyn as Roslyn Taber in *The Misfits*. Arthur Miller wrote the role for Marilyn, as their marriage fell apart. Their strained relationship and their presence on the sweltering Reno, Nevada, set only increased the tension of the troubled shoot. Marilyn's health, both mental and physical, was deteriorating rapidly and she was consuming large quantities of the sleeping pill Nembutal. She was often late or absent due to "illness," and, in the middle of the shoot, she was hospitalized with an emotional breakdown, forcing director John Huston to shut down the production for a week.

Opposite: *The Misfits* (1961). Pictured are (front row, from left) Montgomery Clift, Marilyn, Clark Gable, (back row, from left) Eli Wallach, screenwriter Arthur Miller, and Director John Huston. Wrote Paul V. Beckly in the New York *Herald Tribune*, "After the long drought of vital American pictures one can now cheer, for *The Misfits* is so distinctly American nobody but an American could have made it. To be honest, I'm not sure anybody could have made it except John Huston from an original script by Arthur Miller, and it is hard to believe Miller could have written it without Marilyn Monroe."

Right: Two troubled stars, Montgomery Clift and Marilyn, in *The Misfits*. Clift drank vodka and grapefruit juice from a thermos on the set, and Marilyn popped sleeping pills. Naturally, they bonded during the grueling shoot. Marilyn commented, "He's the only person I know who's in worse shape than I am."

ight: With Clark Gable in a
scene from *The Misfits*. The
New York *Daily News* review
stated, "Gable has never done
anything better on the screen,
nor has Miss Monroe."

eft: Marilyn and Clark Gable
say their good-byes at the
end of filming *The Misfits*. It
would be the last complete
movie for both stars. Ironically,
Gable commented at the time,
regarding Marilyn and the
shoot, "Christ, I'm glad this picture's finished. She damn near
gave me a heart attack." The
day after he left the set, Gable
did indeed suffer a massive
coronary, and ten days later,
on November 16, 1960, he was
dead.

Above: Marilyn and Montgomery Clift at the Loew's Capitol Theatre in New York for the premiere of *The Misfits*. Said Marilyn of her co-star, "That man is beautiful, but he's killing himself slowly. Or not so slowly." Clift would outlive Marilyn, but not by much. In 1966, at the age of forty-five, Clift died of heart failure, brought about by abuse of alcohol and drugs.

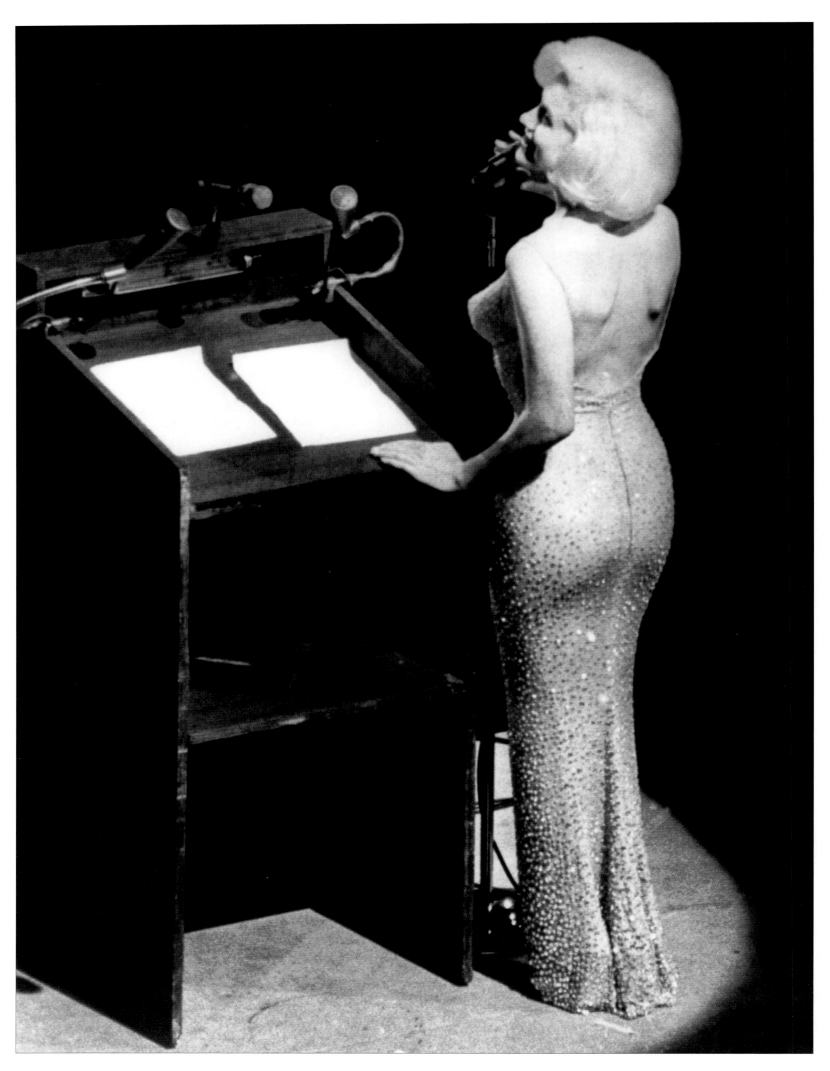

Opposite: On May 19, 1962, at Madison Square Garden, Marilyn, filled with champagne and dressed in a revealing sequined gown, sang a breathy, seductive "Happy Birthday" to President John F. Kennedy. After her performance, the President took the stage and commented, "I can now retire from politics after having had 'Happy Birthday' sung to me in such a sweet, wholesome way." It is widely rumored that Marilyn had affairs with both John and Robert Kennedy (then the Attorney General). She is quoted as having said, "I made it with the Prez," and, regarding his brother, "Bobby Kennedy promised to marry me." The true nature of her relationship to the Kennedys, however, remains a mystery.

Above: This haunting image of Marilyn from July 18, 1962, was, according to photographer George Barris, the last taken of the screen goddess before her death from a drug overdose. Her body language and facial expression, and the grainy, veiled appearance of the photograph combine to suggest a woman who has turned inward and found a great and familiar sadness there.

Above: Throngs of fans stood outside the gates of Westwood Park Memorial Chapel on August 8, 1962, to pay their last regards to Marilyn Monroe. Inside, Lee Strasberg delivered the eulogy: "Others were as physically beautiful as she was, but there was obviously something more in her, something that people saw and recognized in her performances and with which they identified."

Left: Joe DiMaggio comforts Marilyn's one-time foster parents, Mr. and Mrs. Sam Kindelcamp, at Marilyn's funeral on August 8, 1962. Said DiMaggio, "It was Hollywood that destroyed her—she was a victim of her friends."

Above: Joe DiMaggio would place fresh flowers at Marilyn's crypt for years after her death.

Conclusion

At Marilyn Monroe's funeral, on August 8, 1962, friend and mentor Lee Strasberg read the following eulogy. It is reproduced here because it sums up so eloquently the mysterious combination of sensuality and innocence, of talent and tragedy, that has made Marilyn so irresistible to successive generations of admirers.

Despite the heights and brilliance she attained on the screen, she was planning for the future: she was looking forward to participating in...many exciting things.... In her eyes and in mine, her career was just beginning. The dream of her talent, which she had nurtured as a child, was not a mirage. When she first came to me I was amazed at the startling sensitivity which she possessed and which had remained fresh and undimmed, struggling to express itself despite the life to which she had been subjected. Others were as physically beautiful as she was, but there was obviously something more in her, something that people saw and recognized in her performances and with which they identified. She had a luminous quality—a combination of wistfulness, radiance, yearning—[that] set her apart and yet made everyone wish to be part of it.... [She was] at once so shy and yet so vibrant. This quality was even more evident when she was on the stage. I am truly sorry that the public who loved her did not have the opportunity to see her as we did, in many of the roles that foreshadowed what she would have become. Without a doubt she would have been one of the really great actresses on the stage.

Above: "If we learn from the life of Marilyn Monroe, she will live on in us."
—Gloria Steinem

Opposite: "I am not interested in money. I just want to be wonderful."
—Marilyn Monroe

Filmography

Scudda Hoo! Scudda Hay! (1948)
Comedy/drama, 95 min, color
Director: F. Hugh Herbert

Ladies of the Chorus (1949)
Musical/romance, 61 min, black & white
Director: Phil Karlson

Love Happy (1949)
Comedy, 91 min, black & white
Director: David Miller

A Ticket to Tomahawk (1950)
Western/comedy, 90 min, color
Director: Richard Sale

The Asphalt Jungle (1950)
Crime, 112 min, black & white
Director: John Huston

The Fireball (1950)
Drama, 84 min, black & white
Director: Tay Garnett

All About Eve (1950)
Drama, 138 min, black & white
Director: Joseph L. Mankiewicz

Right Cross (1950)
Drama, 90 min, black & white
Director: John Sturges

Hometown Story (1951)
Drama, 61 min, black & white
Director: Arthur Pierson

As Young as You Feel (1951)
Comedy, 77 min, black & white
Director: Harmon Jones

Love Nest (1951)
Comedy, 84 min, black & white
Director: Joseph M. Newman

Let's Make It Legal (1951)
Comedy, 77 min, black & white
Director: Richard Sale

Clash by Night (1952)
Drama, 105 min, black & white
Director: Fritz Lang

We're Not Married (1952)
Comedy, 85 min, black & white
Director: Edmund Goulding

Don't Bother to Knock (1952)
Thriller, 76 min, black & white
Director: Roy Baker

Monkey Business (1952)
Comedy, 97 min, black & white
Director: Howard Hawks

O. Henry's Full House (1952)
Comedy/drama, 117 min, black & white
Directors: Henry Hathaway,
Howard Hawks, Henry King,
Henry Koster, Jean Negulesco

Niagara (1953)
Thriller, 89 min, color
Director: Henry Hathaway

Gentlemen Prefer Blondes (1953)
Musical, 91 min, color
Director: Howard Hawks

How to Marry a Millionaire (1953)
Comedy, 95 min, color
Director: Jean Negulesco

River of No Return (1954)
Western, 91 min, color
Director: Otto Preminger

There's No Business Like Show Business
(1954)
Musical, 117 min, color
Director: Walter Lang

The Seven Year Itch (1955)
Comedy, 105 min, color
Director: Billy Wilder

Bus Stop (1956)
Comedy, 96 min, color
Director: Joshua Logan

The Prince and the Showgirl (1957)
Comedy, 117 min, color
Director: Laurence Olivier

Some Like It Hot (1959)
Crime/comedy, 119 min, black & white
Director: Billy Wilder

Let's Make Love (1960)
Musical/comedy, 118 min, color
Director: George Cukor

The Misfits (1961)
Western, 124 min, black & white
Director: John Huston

Bibliography

Carpozi, George, Jr. *Marilyn Monroe: Her Own Story*. New York: Belmont Books, 1961.

Conway, Michael, and Mark Ricci. *The Films of Marilyn Monroe*. New York: The Citadel Press, 1964.

Goode, James. *The Story of the Misfits*. New York: Bobbs-Merrill, 1963.

Guiles, Fred L. *Legend: The Life and Death of Marilyn Monroe*. New York: Stein and Day, 1984.

Harvey, Diana Karanikas, and Jackson Harvey. *Dead Before Their Time*. New York: Friedman/Fairfax Publishers, 1996.

Hudson, James A. *The Mysterious Death of Marilyn Monroe*. New York: Voliant Books, 1968.

Mailer, Norman. *Marilyn*. New York: Grosset & Dunlap, 1973.

Pepitone, Lena, and William Stadiem. *Marilyn Monroe Confidential*. New York: Simon & Schuster, 1979.

Reies, Randall, and Neal Hitchens. *The Unabridged Marilyn: Her Life from A to Z*. New York: Congdon & Weed, Inc., 1987.

Slatzer, Robert. *The Life and Curious Death of Marilyn Monroe*. New York: Pinnacle Books, 1974.

Spada, James, with George Zeno. *Monroe: Her Life in Pictures*. New York: Doubleday, 1982.

Spoto, Donald. *Marilyn Monroe, The Biography*. New York: HarperCollins Publishers, 1993.

Steinem, Gloria. *Marilyn*. New York: Henry Holt and Company, 1986.

Summers, Anthony. *Goddess: The Secret Lives of Marilyn Monroe*. New York: Macmillan, 1985.

Taylor, Roger. *Marilyn Monroe: In Her Own Words*. New York: Delilah/Putnam, 1983.

Watson, Delmar, and Paul Arnold. *Goin' Hollywood, 1887–1987*. Hollywood: Delmar Watson, 1987.

Zolotow, Maurice. *Marilyn Monroe*. New York: Harcourt Brace, 1960.

Photography Credits

Index